Heart and Soul

Velisa Oliver

Copyright © 2020 by Velisa Oliver.

ISBN-978-1-6485-8192-2

All rights reserved. No part of this book may be reproduced or transmitted in any form or by any means, electronic or mechanical, including photocopying, recording, or by any information storage and retrieval system, without permission in writing from the copyright owner.

The views expressed in this work are solely those of the author and do not necessarily reflect the views of the publisher, and the publisher hereby disclaims any responsibility for them.

Matchstick Literary
1-888-306-8885
orders@matchliterary.com

Table of Contents

Shelter In The Storm 1
Jesus Is The Rock 2
Stand 3
God's Plan 4
God's Timing 5
Never Alone 6
Alive In Christ 7
Redeemed 8
Forgiveness 9
King Jesus 10
Walk In the Light 11
Find Your Way 12
Forget The Past 13
Breakthrough 14
The Process 15
Run Your Race 16
A Grateful Heart 17
Broken Pieces 18
To Know God 19
Closed Door 20
When You Touch 21

Leading You Back To Me 22
Open Door 23
Cleanse Me 24
Joy and Pain 25
Seek My Face 26
God's Will 27
Revelation Of The Heart.. 28

Shelter In The Storm

When the paths of life take you through twist and turns
Jesus will be right there he is closer than you think
The lord will keep you safe from harm
He will not allow you to sink

Surely as the rain falls from up above
The lord will shelter you through the storm
With all of his love

Jesus Is The Rock

Jesus your name is above all names
You are a lily in the valley
You're also joy in the midst of my pain

You are the bright and morning star
No matter the situation
You'll meet us wherever we are

Lord you are my hope
When things around me seem to go wrong
You will carry me in your arms
And help me to be strong
Jesus you are my rock all day long

Stand

When you're going through trials and tribulations
That this world will sometimes bring
Try not to worry or be fearful
But instead put on the garment of praise and sing

God will fight your battles from beginning to the end
He will give you strength to stand
And when it's over and done
You know that you will win

God's Plan

Before you were born and still in your mother's womb
God knew the plans that he would have for each of you

I do believe that we are all born with a purpose
And have a destiny to fulfill
But it's up to each individual to make a choice
To seek after the father's will

Sometimes in life we want to follow our own plan
God knows what's best for us
Because he created every single man

God's Timing

Have you been praying and calling out to God
For an answer to your prayer?

There are problems that you need to be fixed
But it seems as though he does not even care
This could be a test that you are going through
Maybe his goal is to build your faith
Until he decides to answer you

No matter what his timing is always right
God will show up when you least expect
Sometimes even in the middle of the night

Never Alone

You and I were never meant to be on our own
When Jesus ascended to heaven he did not leave us alone
He gave us the Holy Spirit
Who lives deep within your heart

The spirit will lead and help to guide the way
If you let him take the part
So before you seek advice elsewhere
And tempted to pick up the phone
Call on the Holy Spirit because
You are never alone

Alive In Christ

Once you have received Jesus as Lord and Savior
He now abides with you
So expect the blessings to come
Along with his favor

Old things have passed away
You're becoming a new creation day by day
In serving him try to do your best
Don't worry about what others or saying
Just be concerned with passing the test

Redeemed

Do we really understand what it means to sacrifice
That's what Jesus did and it was such a hefty price

The blood that he shed is what makes us free
It came streaming down the cross
From the top of Calvary
To pay off to restore
To save to atone for
You and I have been redeemed
All of the above stated is exactly
What it means

Forgiveness

We must all learn to forgive
When others mistreat or do us wrong
If you're having a hard time forgiving
Pray and ask the father to help
He'll give you strength to be strong

To carry around unforgiveness in the heart
You may not realize it right now but
Sooner or later it only tears you apart

So let it go and be the end
Make peace with the person and
The healing process will begin

King Jesus

Jesus you are the one and only true king
Many in this world have given themselves
A title claiming to be the same thing

You rule and reign with all
Power in your hands
You're sovereign and merciful
All the earth belongs to you
As well as the land

Jesus you are the one and only true king

Walk In the Light

A message to the children of God
Walk in the light have nothing to do
With the evil things of this world
And stand for what you know is right

You don't have to follow the crowd
Just to fit in
Because once this earthly life is over
The eternal life begins

Find Your Way

For those of you who have gone astray
You've been sinking deep in sin
And have lost your way
It's never too late to start over again

Jesus will meet you night or day
All you need is to find your way

When a son or daughter returns back home
All the angels in heaven start to rejoice
As for you they'll be no regrets because
You know that it was the right choice

Forget The Past

Once you've made a choice to answer the call
Keep your eyes straight ahead
There will be distractions all around
That may just cause you to stumble and fall

You must forget the past if you're to move ahead
You can't take it with you
Leave the past behind
Because your past is now dead

Breakthrough

At times it may seem like God is nowhere to be found
Life is chaotic and troubles have gotten you down
Don't worry he is always right there
Watching and listening to every prayer

You've had just about all that you can take
Be still and wait because he will show up
Right at the moment you are about to break

Thank him even when you don't see any sign
Your breakthrough will come in the nick of time

The Process

If you truly want to be used by God
There's a process that every servant
Has to go through that you can't avoid

He will begin to purge and take things out of you
God has to prepare and get you ready for
The assignment he's called you to do

The process may cause you a little pain
But once he's done preparing you
You'll have so much more to gain

Run Your Race

On your mark, get set, ready go
Every believer must run their race
Don't get too far ahead of God
Or lag too far behind him
Just keep up with his pace

God will help you to overcome
The obstacles along the way
Make your crooked paths straight
While on the journey day to day

There may be times you will fall down
But get up and back in the race
So when you get to the finish line
You will be given your jeweled crown

A Grateful Heart

A grateful heart is filled with so much joy
Always willing to help others when in need
Whether it's a man, woman, girl, or boy

A grateful heart does not mind giving back
Sharing their resources or time with other's
For this reason a grateful heart shall not lack

Broken Pieces

In this life we will all experience things
That can cause so much hurt and pain
It maybe our fault sometimes or other's
It does not matter because God can
Take away all of the guilt and shame

If you would be honest and open
With him when you start to pray
Then the healing power of God
Will come in and begin right away

He can put the broken pieces
Of life back together again
What was torn he will now mend

To Know God

To know God is a wonderful thing
The angels bow down before him
To worship and they also sing

He is merciful, loving and kind
Anytime we are in trouble
God comes to our rescue
To get us out of a bind

I love you with all of my heart
Thank you for sending us Jesus
Who gives us grace and mercy
A life also with a brand new start

Closed Door

When a door does not open there is a reason why
You've done everything you know how
And gave it your best try

When an obstacle pops up in your way every time
Take it as a warning that God is sending you a sign

Do you ever stop and think maybe he has closed the door
God knows what's best for you
And probably has something better instore

When You Touch

Lord a simple touch from you can make me whole
Just as you gave sight to the blind man
You are able to heal anyone's soul

When you speak your voice can
Calm the waves in a raging sea
And when the storms are raging
In my life you'll do the same for me

Leading You Back To Me

If you hear my voice calling
And feel me knocking at your heart
I am extending you an invitation
Waiting to give you a brand new start

I will help you to carry the heavy load you bear
My yoke is easy and my burden is light
That is because I really do care

My child I am leading you back to me
Together we will take this journey
What an adventure it will be

Open Door

When you obey the voice of God
And follow his every command
You are surrendering to his will
He's going to lead you by the hand

At the right time he will place an open door
By faith you must walk through
It is the blessing you've been praying for
And now it has finally come to you

Cleanse Me

Lord as I kneel down before you here in prayer
Search my heart and remove what should not be there

Let the fire of your Holy Spirit
Cleanse me from the inside out
Burning up every impure thing
So that I may please and serve
You faithfully without a doubt

Joy and Pain

It is often said no pain no gain
Just as God will cause the sun to shine
In your life he will also send some rain

God desires for us to trust and depend
On him alone and not in the material
Things or worldly riches because
At any moment they can all be gone

Once you understand the purpose for the pain
Then you'll appreciate the end result of the gain

Seek My Face

To those of you who are wandering
Seek my face while you still can
Tomorrow is not promised to you
Or the end of day for any living man

It is not my will that any man
Should perish or lose his soul
Chasing after fame and fortune
In a dying world if the truth be told

God's Will

God's will is the safest place for any of us to be
He watches carefully over his children and
Helps them to fulfill their place of destiny

He will provide what is needed
To carry out his will and when
The path you're on does not
Seem clear he is going to speak
All you need is to listen and if
He say's to wait just be still

Revelation Of The Heart

God will always speak
When he does he speaks to the heart

You must pay close attention to hear
And drown out every other voice
To be able to tell them apart

The revelation that he gives
Is always to encourage you
It helps you to see things
More clearly when you
Don't have a simple clue

www.ingramcontent.com/pod-product-compliance
Lightning Source LLC
Chambersburg PA
CBHW060345080526
44584CB00013B/921